MOUNTAIN BIKING

AILEEN WEINTRAUB

HIGH
interest
books

Children's Press®
A Division of Scholastic Inc.
New York / Toronto / London / Auckland / Sydney
Mexico City / New Delhi / Hong Kong
Danbury, Connecticut

Book Design: Michael DeLisio
Contributing Editor: Scott Waldman
Photo Credits: Cover, pp. 12, 20, 23, 25 © Tony Donaldson/Icon SMI/Rosen
Publishing; back cover, p. 18 © Duomo/Corbis; title page, p. 3 © Corbis; pp. 5,
11, 16, 26, 28, 31 © STL/Icon SMI; p. 6 © Bettmann/Corbis; p. 8 © Museum of
History & Industry/Corbis; p. 15 © Larry Stanley/Index Stock Imagery, Inc.;
p. 24 © Robert Huser/Index Stock Imagery, Inc.; p. 32 © Frank Staub/Index
Stock Imagery, Inc.; p. 34 © Allen Russell/Index Stock Imagery, Inc.; p. 36
© Scott McDermott/Corbis; p. 39 © Paul Gallaher/Index Stock Imagery, Inc.

Library of Congress Cataloging-in-Publication Data

Weintraub, Aileen, 1973-
    Mountain biking / Aileen Weintraub.
    v. cm. -- (X-treme outdoors)
    Includes index.
    Contents: X-treme beginnings -- The thrill of it all --
    Taking your rig for a spin -- Get out there!
    ISBN 0-516-24321-7 (lib. bdg.) -- ISBN 0-516-24384-5 (pbk.)
    1. All terrain cycling--Juvenile literature. [1. All terrain
    cycling.] I. Title. II. Series.

GV1056 .W45 2003
796.6'3--dc21

                                          2002008598

CONTENTS

INTRODUCTION

You're tearing down a steep slope on your brand new mountain bike. It's a gorgeous spring day. You fly past the spruce and fir trees, and through the brush. There's mud splashed all over your clothing. Suddenly, you spot a fallen tree in your path. You do not panic, however. You quickly lift up your handlebars and soar over the tree. A big smile covers your face. You're hooked on the thrill of mountain biking.

Mountain biking has been called an *X-treme* sport. *X-treme* sports are challenging—and dangerous. They require learning highly technical skills. However, if you are looking for adventure and want to test your limits, then mountain biking may be for you.

Mountain biking is challenging, but it can also be done safely. You can join competitions, race with others, or you can simply free ride. Free riding is the most popular type of mountain biking. There are no races or strenuous hill climbs. It's just you on your bike, riding through the woods and looking for adventure. Mountain biking involves riding your bike on dirt trails or roads. It doesn't even have to be done on mountains. The trails mountain bikers follow are only wide enough for one or two people. Some mountain bike trails, called singletracks, are not much wider than a bike tire. Regardless of where you ride, you will find adventure.

Mountain biking can take you places you'd never be able to reach in a single day's hike. Found a great fishing spot? It's probably easy to get to on a bike. Looking for a quiet spot in the woods? Perhaps you simply want to get away from civilization for a while. No problem. Just hop on your bike for a ride through nature's beauty.

What type of person becomes hooked on mountain biking? Where did this *X-treme* sport get its start? What kind of equipment do you need? Are there clubs you can join? Hop on board for a ride through the exciting world of mountain biking!

Mountain biking is a great way to explore the wilderness.

CHAPTER ONE

X-TREME BEGINNINGS

Mountain biking is believed to date back to about 1896. The U.S. Army wanted to see if bikes could be used as a means to travel the rough land of the West. A group of African American soldiers rode on bikes from Missoula, Montana, around Yellowstone Park, and then over the Rocky Mountains to St. Louis, Missouri. The trip was over 1,900 miles (3,058 kilometers). At the time, most African American soldiers were known as buffalo soldiers. They were given this name by Native Americans who thought the soldiers were as brave and fearless as the buffalo. These early mountain bikers made up the 25th Infantry Bicycle Corps. It was the only time the U.S. Army ever had a corps of bicyclists.

In the 1950s, the Velo Cross Club Parisien of France developed a sport similar to mountain biking.

Buffalo soldiers were in charge of settling some of the wildest areas of the American West. They explored and built roads through some of the harshest terrain in the United States.

There were few paved roads for early bicyclists, such as this man, in the early 1900s. However, people didn't start taking their bikes onto mountain trails until the 1950s.

The twenty young bicyclists in this club added suspension, stronger brakes, and handlebar-mounted gearshifts to their 650-B bikes. This made their bikes more "mountain-ready." The men raced their bikes on outdoor dirt tracks during breaks at French motorcycle races.

John Finley Scott is considered to be one of the first mountain bikers in the United States. In 1953, Scott took an old Schwinn bike frame and added nine gears to it. He also added flat handlebars, stronger brakes, and fat balloon tires. Scott called his new invention a Woodsie Bike. Unfortunately, Scott's enthusiasm for the new sport did not catch on with many other bikers.

Many mountain biking enthusiasts claim that mountain biking as we now know it got its start in 1974. Gary Fisher of Marin County, California, was a bicycle mechanic. He made modifications to a 1940s bike and added thick balloon tires. He called the bike a Clunker. He built the bike especially to handle rough, off-road terrain. By 1979, Fisher and some friends were making and selling these Clunkers for $1,500 each. Mountain bikes became widely available in 1982 across the country when the Specialized Bicycle Company began selling mountain bikes.

Years of testing and research have enabled bike makers to produce sleeker and lighter bikes than ever before. Today's bikes are built with state-of-the-art technology, such as powerful brakes and strong, lightweight bicycle frames. Handlebars are flatter and stick straight out so riders can sit in an upright position. Riders can now strap their feet onto the pedals with mechanical clamps so that they aren't bounced off their bike on harsh terrain.

The addition of suspension made for a better ride, too. Suspension is a system of springs on the bike that absorb the shock of riding on the road. With better suspension, mountain bikers can ride longer without tiring their arms. It also makes for a much smoother ride, which is easier on a rider's wrists. Modern mountain bikes are safer and more fun to ride than ever.

X-FACTOR

For those who live for mountain biking, there's the Mountain Bike Hall of Fame located in Crested Butte, Colorado. This museum was founded in 1988. It is home to vintage bikes, press clippings, and photos of historical races.

Suspension

Fork

There are many different types of bike suspension. On this bike, the suspension is located just above the fork.

CHAPTER TWO

THE THRILL OF IT ALL

People from many different walks of life enjoy mountain biking. Many of them believe that wilderness areas make for the most enjoyable biking experience. With the proper clothing and equipment, mountain biking can be done year round. All you really need is a bike, a helmet, and some common sense.

RULES OF THE TRAIL

It's important to ride safely at all times and to be polite to others on the trail. Before hitting the trails, know the basics. The International Mountain Biking Association (IMBA) has set the following rules.

Mountain bikes are built to withstand even the toughest trails.

- **Ride on open trails.** Do not trespass on private property. If you need a permit to ride on a trail, get it in advance.
- **Leave no trace.** Don't skid your tires. This causes damage to the trails. Riding through muddy trails also causes erosion of the soil.
- **Control your bike.** Obey speed laws. Slow down when you see others on the trail.
- **Yield the trail to others.** Signal to other people that you're on the path. Try a friendly greeting or a bell. Be prepared to stop at any time. Always give way to people on horses and uphill bike traffic.
- **Never scare animals.** Allow animals on the trail to adjust to your presence. Give them plenty of space. Keep loud noises to a minimum. You can cause a dangerous situation by frightening an animal.
- **Plan ahead.** Be prepared by knowing your equipment and knowing your limitations.

Only ride on trails on which you feel comfortable. Get off your bike and walk in areas that seem too dangerous, such as steep downhill slopes or rocky passes.

Even the most experienced mountain bikers walk their bikes through the difficult parts of a trail.

If you're biking with friends, ask them not to get too far ahead of you. A relaxed, enjoyable day on the trail should not become a wild racing event. Take a lot of rest stops along the way. The more tired you become, the harder it will be to concentrate on your riding. Remember, using common sense will ensure a great day on the trail.

Finding a mountain bike that you are comfortable riding will make your day on the trail much easier.

HITTING THE TRAIL

Your main piece of equipment is, of course, a mountain bike. You'll want a bike made especially for mountain trails. The bike should have fat, knobby tires and a strong frame. Most bike frames are made of aluminum, carbon fiber, steel, or titanium. Full suspension bikes, which have suspension on the front and back wheels, are the most expensive. On rough terrain, however, they save a lot of wear and tear on your body.

Shop around to get a good deal on the bike that's best for you. Talk to the experts who have been mountain biking for a while. Ask them a lot of questions. It's also a good idea to test ride at least three different bikes. This will give you a better idea of the bike on which you are most comfortable. You can even search the Internet for great deals. As a first-time mountain biker, you may want to consider buying a used bike. A used bike can cost less, but be sure that it's in good shape. Take a test ride. Then have a bike mechanic give it a good look, too.

GETTING IN GEAR

HELMET

Wearing a helmet is an absolute must. A good helmet can save your life. Make sure to buy one that fits well. Your helmet should be lightweight and well ventilated. Look for the Consumer Product Safety Commission (CPSC) stamp of approval. Snell certification is also a good sign. Snell certification is given by the Snell Memorial Foundation after the helmet has passed the toughest safety-testing standards in the world.

GLOVES

Riding gloves will keep you from compressing the nerves in your hands. Gloves are also good for preventing blisters. Should you fall (and you probably will!), gloves will save your skin from some nasty scrapes.

BICYCLE SHORTS

Find padded bicycle shorts that fit more snugly than regular shorts. Their padding will make your ride a lot more comfortable.

Many bike stores sell a full range of biking equipment that will make your ride safe, as well as comfortable.

MOUNTAIN BIKE SHOES

Mountain bike shoes provide stiff sole support when you're pedaling. If you're a beginner, lightweight hiking boots will work well, too.

PROTECTIVE GLASSES

Glasses will protect your eyes from ever-present road hazards, such as bugs, twigs, dirt, and pebbles bouncing off the road. They also protect your eyes from the sun and wind.

CLOTHING

Dress for the weather. It is always colder on the top of a mountain than it is below. Dressing in layers is a good idea. Check the weather conditions before hitting the trail to avoid any surprises. Synthetic fabrics are better for outdoor use than cotton. Cotton will not keep you warm when it's wet, and it also takes a long time to dry out. Many synthetic fabrics are designed to pull moisture, such as rain and sweat, from your body.

Allen wrenches

Gloves

Water bottle

valve tube
26 x 1.75-2.35
WRENCH FORCE

Spare tube

Helmet

Mountain bike shoes

Air pump

Accessory bag

Glasses

Tire iron

Pack enough food and water for the day. You burn a lot of calories riding a mountain bike. Drink plenty of water, so that you don't get dehydrated. Also, bring along a basic first aid kit. Other accessories that you may want to take on your adventure are a map, a compass, and matches in a waterproof container. If you're going to be out after sunset, bring along a head-lamp, which attaches to your helmet.

FIXING YOUR RIG

At some point your bike will most likely need to be repaired. Knowing how to make your own repairs may save you some money—and headaches. You should know how to fix a flat tire. Be prepared to fix a derailed or broken chain. Know what to do with broken spokes. Many riders keep repair items in a pouch that fits below their seat.

Air Pump Make sure to have a pump that will fit your valve type. Try a light, compact pump.

Spare Tube You'll need one if you get a flat on the trail. It will keep you on the trail until you can patch the flat at home.

A smart mountain biker wears the right clothing and packs the proper equipment for a day on the trail.

21

Patch Kit Keep a kit on hand in case you get another flat after using your spare tube.

Tire Irons You will need tire irons to help remove the tire when changing the tube.

Major repairs should be done at a bike shop by an experienced mechanic. Basic maintenance can be done at least once a month if you keep your bike in tip-top shape. People who ride a lot do maintenance more frequently.

You should know how to take care of your bike yourself. Some simple maintenance tasks to learn include:

- Cleaning and lubricating the chain
- Checking and adjusting the tire pressure
- Adjusting the brakes
- Tightening the bolts
- Checking the wheels for alignment
- Cleaning the bike frame
- Lubricating the cables and the derailleur, which shifts the gears

Bike mechanics use a variety of tools to keep mountain bikes pedaling in tip-top shape.

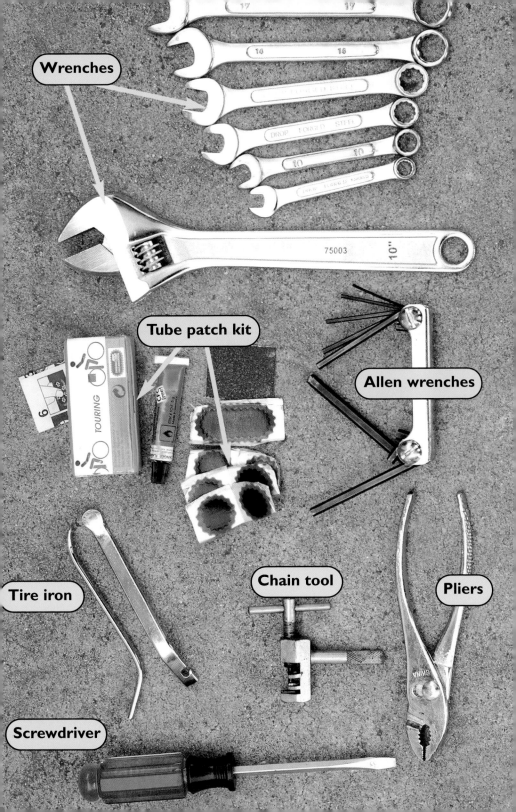

Wrenches

Tube patch kit

Allen wrenches

Tire iron

Chain tool

Pliers

Screwdriver

Always check your brakes before riding. Good brakes make for a safe, enjoyable ride. If they're not working well, try cleaning the wheel rims with rubbing alcohol and steel wool. You can also take a piece of light sandpaper and sand the brake pads until they have a rough texture. If the brakes still don't work the way that you would like, take the bike into the shop and have the brakes replaced or tuned. One of the most important aspects of bike safety is having a set of brakes that works properly.

Seat

Handlebars

Spokes

Fork

Rim

Suspension

Derailleur

Pedal

Hub

When you squeeze the brake lever on your handlebars, the brake pads squeeze the rim of the tire to stop the bike.

CHAPTER THREE

TAKING YOUR RIG FOR A SPIN

GETTING IN SHAPE

Mountain biking will be a lot more fun, and safer, if you're in good physical shape. Upper- and lower-body strength is key to mountain biking. Do push-ups, pull-ups, and deep knee bends to prepare yourself. Strengthening your upper body will help you balance your weight while riding. Upper-body strength also makes it easier to lift up your front tire as you ride over obstacles, such as rocks and logs. Strong lower-body muscles will help power you up steep hills.

As a beginner, you're going to want to take it easy on your first couple of runs. Go slowly. Get to know how your bike handles around turns and over obstacles. You will want to build up experience before

Upper-body strength will prepare you for the challenges of the trail.

As you ride down steep downhill terrain, form is important. These riders are showing good form by leaning backward and keeping their legs bent.

taking on steep climbs and rugged terrain. Try biking with people more experienced than yourself. You'll be able to learn quickly by watching what they do and by asking them questions.

Stay relaxed as you learn to ride. Practice shifting your gears a lot. For steep uphill climbs, use your granny gear. This is the easiest gear on your bike and offers the least resistance for pedaling. Keep up your momentum while you climb. Don't stop and try to start again. Believe it or not, it's easier to struggle up a hill without stopping, than it is to keep stopping and starting over and over. Stay seated, but lean forward. This will provide your bike with better traction. Eventually, you may decide that you prefer to stand up on steep or slippery climbs. Rock the bike gently back and forth to keep your tires in a straight line. Rock to the right as your right pedal goes down. Rock to the left as your left pedal goes down.

When going downhill, keep your weight toward the back and bend your knees. You don't need to pedal. Concentrate on steering and working your brakes. If you can't avoid a major obstacle, like a log, pull up on your handlebars. This will cause your front wheel to lift off the ground. Then your back wheel should roll right over the obstacle. Be careful not to hit anything too hard because you could bend your spokes or tire rims.

There are four key aspects to mountain biking that you should practice before taking on very tough trails:

Balance Good balance is the key to successful mountain biking. If you feel your back wheel slipping, move back on your seat. If you're in a standing position, put more weight on the rear of the bike by leaning backward. If your front wheel starts coming off the ground, add weight to it by leaning forward.

Cornering Focus on where you want to go, not what you are afraid of hitting. Lean into turns. Brake before cornering, not during it.

Braking Most brake force is in the front of the bike. Avoid locking your back brakes. It can cause bad skids. It's also not very effective in slowing you down.

Shifting Lower gears spin on hills more easily, making a tough climb more manageable. Shift to a lower gear before you come to the middle of a steep hill.

WORKING WITH THE ELEMENTS

As a mountain biker, you need to be aware of all the obstacles that will cross your path. Here are some things to watch out for:

Learning how to deal with many different types of trails will make you a much stronger rider.

- **Mud** Don't ride through it. It causes erosion on the trails. If the mud is deep, walk your bike around it. Don't ride around it. This will cause the trail to widen.
- **Rocks, Holes, and Bumps** Move your weight back so your front wheel can float over these obstacles. You may need to lift your front wheel.
- **Water** Try not to ride through streams. If you have no choice, ride through in a low gear.

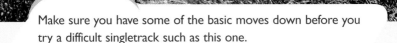

Make sure you have some of the basic moves down before you try a difficult singletrack such as this one.

As you become more experienced on your mountain bike, obstacles will actually become part of the fun. Mountain bikers ride their bikes off-road because they prefer the thrill of rough terrain. Take your time at first as you get used to riding over obstacles. Before you know it, you'll be rocketing down the mountains just like the pros.

THE SINGLETRACK

A singletrack is a narrow trail, usually sunk down a few inches in the earth. Singletracks are much narrower and steeper than dirt roads. Turns are sharper on a singletrack.

One of the most important things to practice before riding on a singletrack is how to distribute your weight evenly. You need to learn how to balance yourself. This will help you to avoid slipping on steep uphills and going over your handlebars if you hit larger obstacles. Practice balancing your weight by leaning backward on downhills and forward on uphills.

At first singletracks may seem intimidating, but the more you ride them, the easier they will become. With a little experience, these trails can be a lot of fun.

X-FACTOR

The Schwinn Bicycle company made large, fat bike tires as early as 1933. These tires measured 26 inches (66 centimeters) by 2 1/8 inches (5.4 cm). That is a lot bigger than most tires today.

CHAPTER FOUR

GET OUT THERE!

The National Sporting Goods Association (NSGA) keeps track of how many people take part in a wide variety of sports. In 1993, 4.6 million people were mountain bikers. By 1998, the number reached 8.6 million. Today, there are even more mountain bikers out on trails around the world. Most bikers ride for enjoyment and the thrill that a mountain trail offers. Since mountain biking is relatively new, it is just starting to be recognized as a competitive sport on the international level.

BIKING IN THE BIG LEAGUES

X Games are the mini Olympics of *X-treme* sports. People from around the world get together to

Each year the number of people who enjoy mountain biking continues to grow.

This is the beginning of a snow mountain bike race in the X Games. Competitors wear a full-face helmet, as well as knee and elbow pads, in case they crash at 70 miles per hour.

compete in various *X-treme* competitions. The 2000 Winter X Games featured snow mountain biking. In snow mountain biking, racers fly down a ski slope at speeds faster than 70 miles per hour (112 kilometers per hour). Screws are placed in the tires to help give the bikes better traction. The winner of any X Game event receives the title "Most Extreme Athlete on the Planet."

Mountain biking premiered as an Olympic sport in Atlanta, Georgia, in 1996. In the Olympics, mountain biking is called cross-country cycling. The two categories were men's individual and women's individual. Mountain biking returned to the Olympic Games at the 2000 Olympics in Sydney, Australia. With time, different types of mountain biking may be featured in the Olympic games.

MOUNTAIN BIKING MANIA!

As the popularity of mountain biking continues to grow, many new forms of the sport are being created. In endurance races, teammates ride together for 24 hours straight. They may ride for hundreds of miles. There are also 24-hour relay races. Teams of four take turns pedaling around a 10 to 15 mile (16 to 24 km) course as many times as they can in 24 hours. There are also uphill races, downhill races, and timed hill climbs. In uphill races, individual riders race each other to get up steep hills first. In downhill races, riders bolt at such high speeds that they must concentrate on keeping their bike from crashing. In timed climbs, riders compete for the best time. Stage racing combines different types of riding. They may include uphill, downhill, and cross-country riding. Riders earn points for their speed in each stage.

The National Off-Road Bicycle Association (NORBA) organizes over 1,000 mountain biking races in the United States each year. The races are for both amateurs and professionals. There is also a World Mountain Bike Championship held each year for riders. Young mountain bikers, ages ten to eighteen, can participate in the Junior Olympics Mountain Bike Series. Kids up to twelve years old can take part in the Shimano Youth Series. This gives kids an opportunity to race against others their own age.

X-FACTOR

The National Off-Road Bicycle Association (NORBA) was created in 1993. At that time it only had 112 members. Now there are well over 30,000.

WHAT ARE YOU WAITING FOR?

Finding places that teach mountain biking can be tough. The best way to learn how to ride a mountain bike is to get out and ride a lot. Mountain biking clubs and organizations can provide the instruction and tips that will sharpen your skills.

Getting out on trails is the best way to become a better mountain biker.

There are many biking organizations and clubs to help you get involved. The International Mountain Bike Association (IMBA) is an environmentally responsible organization. Members spend time volunteering to maintain trails. The Women's Mountain Bike and Tea Society (Wombats) is an organization dedicated to women bikers. It encourages women to cycle the trails in their area. It's a great way for women to find fun riding partners who have the same goals and expectations.

There are also rider development camps. These camps provide training opportunities for riders. There are a number of magazines and books you can check out if you are interested in learning more about this *X-treme* sport. Check out the back of this book for details, including some great Web sites. After you do your research, get out there and hit the trail! A mountain biking adventure awaits you!

NEW WORDS

alignment to adjust or bring into line

corps a section or branch of the armed forces having a special function

derailleur the mechanism that moves the chain when gears are shifted; there are two derailleurs on a mountain bike, front and rear

erosion the process of wearing away

fork attaches the front wheel to the bike and houses the steerer tube

gear controls the level of pedaling difficulty

gearshift the mechanism used to change the gears on a bike

NEW WORDS

handlebars the bar on a mountain bike used for steering; brakes and gear shifts are mounted on the handlebars

modifications changes or adjustments

rims the metal hoops on which the tubes and tires are mounted

spokes the thin metal cables that connect a wheel's hub to the rim

suspension springs or other devices on bikes that absorb bumps and other jolting movements making the ride feel smoother

synthetic produced artificially

terrain the physical features of land

FOR FURTHER READING

Behr, Steve. *Mountain Biking.* Hauppauge, NY: Barron's Educational Series, 1998.

Berto, Frank J. *The Birth of Dirt: The Origins of Mountain Biking.* San Francisco, CA: Van der Plaas Publications, 1999.

Brouwer, Sigmund. *Mountain Biking...To the Extreme—Cliff Dive.* Nashville, TN: Tommy Nelson, Wordkids, 1996.

Chistopher, Matt. *Mountain Biking Mania.* New York: Little, Brown & Co, 1998.

Demattei, Susan, and Bill Strickland. *Mountain Biking: The Ultimate Guide to the Ultimate Ride.* New York: McGraw-Hill, 1998.

Zinn, Lennard. *Zinn and the Art of Mountain Bike Maintenance.* Boulder, CO: Velo Press, 1998.

RESOURCES

Great Riding Locations in the United States

Acadia National Park, Maine As you ride the 27-mile (43 km) park loop on Maine's Mount Desert Island, you'll have a great view of a seventeen-peak chain of mountains. Cadillac Mountain, at 1,530 feet (466 meters), is the Atlantic Coast's highest point.

Death Valley National Park, California Nine mountain ranges, as well as ghost towns and narrow canyons, surround Death Valley and its many backcountry roads. At Death Valley, you can check out the Native American petroglyphs and get a close look at the canyons' layers.

Moab, Utah Moab has some of the greatest mountain biking in the United States. The Slickrock Trail is one of the most famous mountain bike trails in the entire country. You'll be amazed by the beauty of Moab and its perfect trails.

RESOURCES

Organizations
Adventure Cycling Association
P.O. Box 8308
Missoula, MT 59807
(406) 721-1776
www.adv-cycling.org

Bicycle Federation of America
1818 R Street NW
Washington, DC 20009
(202) 332-6986

International Mountain Biking Association
P.O. Box 7578
Boulder, CO 80306
(303) 545-9011

USA Cycling
One Olympic Plaza
Colorado Springs, CO 80909
(719) 578-4581